THIS WALKER BOOK BELONGS TO:

Maddy

Alphonse

Archie

Georgia

Vikram

Claudia

Ling

Harry

For all the enchanting babies

and toddlers at our music group.

First published 1996 by Walker Books Ltd
87 Vauxhall Walk, London SE11 5HJ

This edition published 1997

4 6 8 10 9 7 5

© 1996 Zita Newcome

This book has been typeset in ITC Highlander Medium

Printed in Hong Kong

British Library Cataloguing in Publication Data
A catalogue record for this book is
available from the British Library.

ISBN 0-7445-5229-X

Toddlerobics is a Registered Trademark™

Toddlerobics

Zita Newcome

WALKER BOOKS
AND SUBSIDIARIES
LONDON • BOSTON • SYDNEY

Hats off, coats off, all rush in,

everybody ready for toddler gym!

Heads and shoulders,

Eyes and ears,

knees and toes.

mouth and nose.

Flap
your
arms
up
and
down.

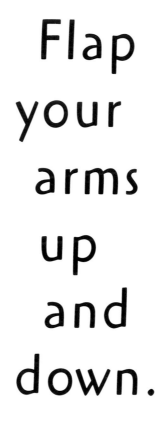

Lift
your
feet
off
the
ground.

Stretch up high
and touch
the sky,

bend down low
and touch
your toes.

Lift that
rattle
in the air,

shake it,

shake it,

everywhere!

Clap your hands,  stamp your feet.

Nod your head,  dance to the beat.

All join together

stretch out your arms

to make a puffer train,

and zoom like a plane.

Make a circle,

Let's bump bottoms,

ring a ring o' roses.

let's
rub
noses.

Sshhh! On tiptoes,

Now great big steps

quiet as a mouse.

all round the house.

Turning,
twirling,
like a
spinning
top.

Bump
on your
bottom
when
it's time
to stop.

Wriggle your toes,

now lie down

crawl like a cat,

and stretch out flat.

Toddlerobics
is lots of fun...

See you next week,
everyone!

Maddy

Alphonse

Archie

Georgia

Vikram

Claudia

Ling

Harry

MORE WALKER PAPERBACKS
For You to Enjoy

THE HAPPY HEDGEHOG BAND
by Martin Waddell/Jill Barton

Deep in the heart of Dickon Wood, Harry and his hedgehog band are
drumming and tumming and making happy music!

"A celebration of noise, admirably conveyed in Jill Barton's illustrations."
The Bookseller

0-7445-3049-0   £4.50

KIDS
by Catherine and Laurence Anholt

"From the absurd to the ridiculous, from the real to the imaginary,
from the nasty to the charming, this is a book which touches on the important
aspects of life as experienced by the young child." *Books for Keeps*

0-7445-6067-5   £4.99

COWS IN THE KITCHEN
by June Crebbin/Katharine McEwen

Cows in the kitchen, ducks on the dresser, pigs in the pantry…
While Tom Farmer snoozes, the animals are whooping it up in the farmhouse!

Adapted from a traditional nonsense song, this rumbustious
picture book is perfect for reading – or singing! – aloud.

0-7445-6947-8   £5.99